SPEED

by Brenda Walpole
Illustrations by Dennis Tinkler
Photographs by Chris Fairclough

Contents

Gareth Stevens Publishing
MILWAUKEE

Hurry up! Get a move on!

Over the centuries, many people have dreamed of being able to travel faster and faster. In ancient legends, some of the gods were famous for their speed. Hermes, the Greek messenger of the gods, had wings on his heels. The Nordic god Thor sped across the sky in a chariot so fast he made claps of thunder.

Why is it important to measure speed?

When traveling by car, you may need to know how long the trip is going to take. This is important so that you can allow enough time to drive at a safe speed.

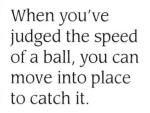

When you've judged the speed of a ball, you can move into place to catch it.

Measuring the speed of someone's heartbeat is one way to check the person's health.

Can you think of any other reasons why we need to measure speed?

Every time we take a measurement of speed, we need to know two things: what has happened, and the time it has taken. A doctor listens to the number of times your heart beats per minute. This is called your heart rate. To measure how fast something is moving, we need to know the distance it has traveled, and the time the trip has taken. We measure the speed of a car in miles or kilometers per hour.

3

Speed on land

To prehistoric people, speed was important for hunting and escaping enemies. Those who could run the fastest were more likely to survive.

Centuries ago, great sporting events called the Olympic Games were organized. This ancient Greek vase shows some long-distance runners competing against each other. The first Olympic Games took place in 776 B.C. in Greece. At these games, the fastest runners were heroes. In 490 B.C., a Greek army messenger ran approximately 25 miles (40 km) from a battle at Marathon to Athens to report a victory. Today, athletes can run in long-distance races called marathons, named in honor of that event.

Even when things travel for just a few seconds or minutes, we can record their speeds in miles or kilometers per hour. The fastest human sprinters can run at speeds of approximately 25 miles (40 km) per hour. The fastest animal, the cheetah, can reach speeds of about 60 miles (100 km) per hour. But neither the sprinter nor the cheetah can keep up these speeds for long. A cheetah may fail to catch prey, such as antelope, because the antelope, though slower than the cheetah, can keep going for a longer time.

Something to try

Find out how fast you walk

You will need:
a measuring stick or tape measure, a stopwatch or a watch with a second hand.

Mark off a distance of 100 yards or meters, or use a running track or sports field that is already measured. For exactly five minutes, walk up and down the track at a comfortable speed. Keep track of how many yards (m) you have walked. Figure out how many yards (m) you would travel in one hour if you kept up the same speed. How many miles (km) per hour is this?

The slowest mammal is the three-toed sloth, which travels only 8 feet (2.43 m) per minute.

To calculate walking and running speeds or the speed of a car, time is measured in minutes or hours and distance in feet (m) or miles (km). Rockets and satellites move so quickly they travel thousands of miles (km) in one hour. Often, their speeds are recorded in miles (km) per second. Which units would you use to measure the speed of a snail?

Every car has a speedometer to show the driver how fast the car is moving. The pointer on the speedometer's dial is connected to the car's engine by a flexible cable. When the driver presses the accelerator, the engine makes the wheels turn faster and cover more ground. The distance traveled by the wheels is converted into miles or kilometers per hour and shown on the speedometer.

The land-speed record, the speed of the fastest car in the world at 633.497 miles (1,019.467 km) per hour, was set by Richard Noble in 1983, driving *Thrust 2*.

Measuring speed in sports

In sports events, when athletes race over a set distance, electronic timing devices are often used to record the speed of the competitors. Sometimes the judges use photographs of the athletes crossing the finish line to help decide the winner.

In downhill ski races, each skier passes through light beams at the starting gate that trigger a timing mechanism. These beams are linked to the control room and a digital display-timer that is accurate to one-hundredth of a second. At the finish line, the skier passes through another beam of light to stop the clock.

Speed on water

The speed of a ship is measured in knots. A ship traveling at one knot covers a distance of one nautical mile per hour. A nautical mile (6,080 ft. or 1,852 m) is longer than a land mile (5,280 ft. or 1.6 m). A nautical mile is a special measure of distance used in the air and on water. It is calculated from a tiny part of the distance of a great circle — a complete circle around Earth, such as the Equator or a line of longitude.

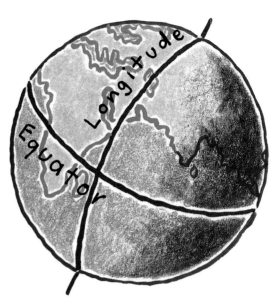

Centuries ago, a ship's speed was measured with a log-line. This was a wooden log attached to a length of rope that was knotted at measured intervals. The rope measured 150 fathoms. A fathom is 6 feet (1.83 m). The rope was wound around a reel on the ship, and the log was thrown overboard. As the ship moved forward, the rope unwound. The number of knots that passed through a sailor's hands in a measured period of time was the ship's speed in knots. The ship's speed was recorded, or logged, in a book called a logbook.

Water speed record: 277.57 knots (319.6 mi. or 514.4 km) per hour, set in 1978 by Kenneth Warby in his hydroplane *Spirit of Australia*.

Make your own log-line for a toy boat

You will need: a toy boat, a pencil that fits loosely
inside a thread spool, thin string, a short twig, clear
tape, modeling clay, a tank or bathtub of water.

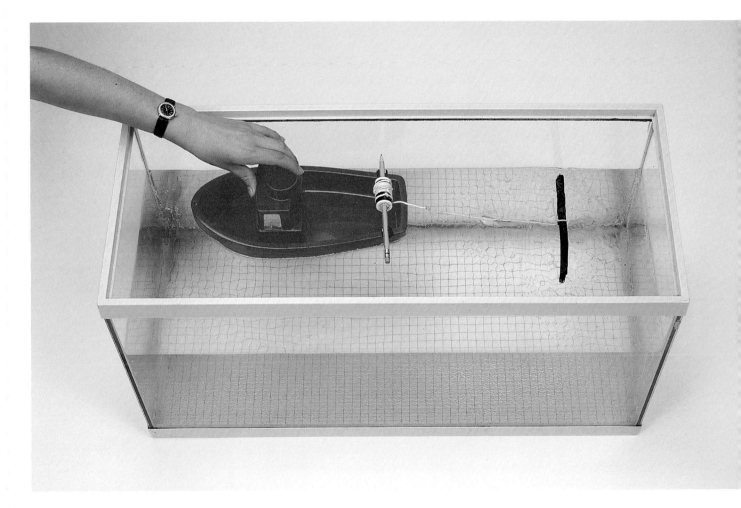

Tie knots in the string at intervals of about 4 inches (10 cm).
Tape one end of the string to the thread spool, and wind the rest
around the spool. Tie the twig to the free end of the string. Feed
the pencil through the middle of the spool and press it firmly onto
small balls of clay on the sides of the boat. Make sure the spool
can turn freely. Float the twig on the water, and gently push the
boat forward. As the spool turns, count how many knots unwind.
If you live near a pond where you can float your boat safely, try to
find out the speed of the boat in knots per minute.

Speed in the air

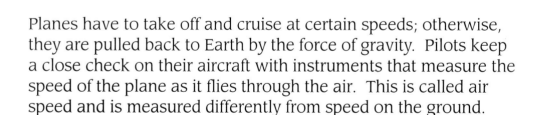

Planes have to take off and cruise at certain speeds; otherwise, they are pulled back to Earth by the force of gravity. Pilots keep a close check on their aircraft with instruments that measure the speed of the plane as it flies through the air. This is called air speed and is measured differently from speed on the ground.

A plane's speed depends on the power of its engines, which give it thrust to move forward and to overcome air resistance that drags it back. Speeding forward gives the plane lift and allows it to take off and climb into the sky. If the plane flies too slowly, it will stall and quickly begin to fall.

Watch the flight path of a paper airplane

Make a paper airplane using the outline at right. Throw it forward as hard as you can. How far does the plane fly before it falls? Throw the plane again with less force so it flies slowly. How far does it fly this time? Note the plane's speed when it stalls and falls to the ground. Can you think of any other reasons why the plane might stall?

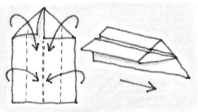

All aircraft have an air speed measurer called a Pitot tube, named after the eighteenth-century scientist Henri Pitot. As an airplane moves forward, the Pitot tube measures the pressure of air rushing into the tube. This information is fed into a computer in the cockpit and shown on a dial as the speed of the plane.

In 1988, the Concorde flew from London to New York in the record time of 2 hours 55 minutes 15 seconds.

As fast as the wind

The direction and strength of the wind are important to pilots because wind affects the speed of the aircraft. At airports, pilots look at wind socks to estimate wind strength and to see in which direction it's blowing.

Something to try

Make your own wind sock

You will need: a bamboo cane or long stick, a nylon knee stocking or nylon sock, thin wire, electrical tape or a stapler, scissors.

Cut off the toe of the stocking and place small hoops of wire at each end. On one hoop, leave a length of wire to push down the middle of the cane or to tape around the stick. Fold one end of the stocking around the wire and staple or tape it in place. Do the same at the other end. Take the wind sock outdoors and stick it in the ground or hold it upright.

As the wind blows, the stocking fills with air and points in the direction the wind is blowing. If the stocking blows out stiffly, the wind is strong. If it hangs loosely, the wind is light.

Meteorologists study the weather. They use instruments called anemometers to record the speed of the wind.

Something to try

Make an anemometer to see how fast the wind blows

You will need: four paper cups, duct tape, two lengths of soft dowel 8 inches (20.3 cm) long and another 12 inches (30.5 cm) long to use as a pole, a flat piece of wood for a base, stones, a dress pin, scissors, a bead.

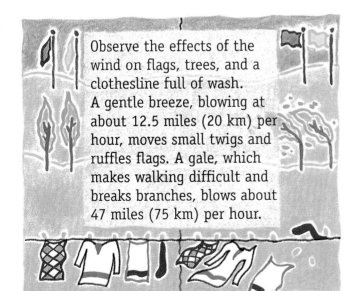

Observe the effects of the wind on flags, trees, and a clothesline full of wash. A gentle breeze, blowing at about 12.5 miles (20 km) per hour, moves small twigs and ruffles flags. A gale, which makes walking difficult and breaks branches, blows about 47 miles (75 km) per hour.

Tape the 8-inch (20-cm) dowels into the shape of a cross. Cut slits in the cups and push them onto the ends of the cross so they face in one direction and make a circle. Push a pin through the middle of the cross, then through the bead and into the pole. The cross should be able to spin freely. Attach the pole to the base with tape or glue. Take your anemometer outside. What happens in a gust of wind?

P.S. Find out about Admiral Sir Francis Beaufort and the scale he invented for judging wind speed.

13

Speeding up, slowing down

On Earth, any machine or living thing needs energy to make it move. You get the energy you need from the food you eat and from oxygen in the air. The food and oxygen are fuel, much like the gasoline a car needs to make it go. Food and oxygen are carried in your blood, which is pumped through your body by your heart. When you exercise, your heart rate and breathing rate speed up to keep your muscles supplied with the fuel they need.

Something to try

See how your heart rate speeds up

Feel the pulse in your wrist with your fingers and count how many times it beats per minute. Then jump rope for awhile and take your pulse again. Rest for a few minutes, then walk briskly for three to five minutes and take your pulse again. Record your results on a chart.

14

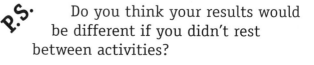

P.S. Do you think your results would be different if you didn't rest between activities?

When a car driver steps down on the accelerator, the car's engine receives more fuel and the car speeds up. Cars carry a reserve of stored energy in a gas tank. If the tank runs out of gas, the car slows down and stops.

Something to try

Make a toy with a reserve of energy wound up in a rubber band

You will need: a plastic bottle, a rubber band, some small pieces of dowel, scissors, a bead, a thin piece of wire.

Make a hole in the base of the bottle and thread one end of the rubber band inside the bottle. Hold the bottom of the loop in place with a piece of dowel. Fish out the other end of the rubber band from the bottle with a wire hook. Thread the rubber band through the bead, which should just fit the bottle neck. Hold the loop in place with the dowel; this is the propeller. Turn the propeller around so it twists the rubber band. Place the bottle on its side and let the propeller go. What happens when the rubber band unwinds?

Friction

On Earth, anything that moves uses energy to overcome friction, the force that slows down moving objects. Friction is caused whenever one moving surface touches another. Objects move fastest on smooth surfaces. You can skate easily on ice but not on concrete. Objects grip onto rough surfaces that cause more friction than smooth ones.

Something to try

Make your own speed test

You will need: a large board, some books, a crayon, an eraser, a coin, a stone, a thread spool, a piece of sandpaper.

Prop one end of the board on some books. Hold the objects at the top of the board and let them all go at the same time. Which object reaches the bottom first? Cover the board with a piece of sandpaper and try the test again. Which surface causes less friction? Can you think how you might speed up the objects?

 P.S. Change the angle of the slope of the board and repeat the test. What happens?

Friction can be reduced by making surfaces smooth. When we want things to move at great speed, such as ice skates or toboggans, we sharpen and wax them. Another way to reduce friction is to cover the surfaces with a thin layer of liquid, called a lubricant. A thin layer of melted ice under an ice skate makes you travel even faster. You travel much faster down a water slide than down a play-ground slide because the water acts as a lubricant.

Oil is a lubricant that is often used in machines with moving parts. As a machine works, the moving parts rub against one another. This slows things down, and the parts begin to wear. Oil helps the parts move faster and stops them from wearing out so quickly.

P.S. Lubricate the board with a little dishwashing liquid and try the speed test again. What happens?

Rolling along

When you want to move an object from one place to another, carrying or dragging it along the ground is slow, hard work. It's quicker and easier to move things on rollers that keep the object off the ground. The huge stones used to build the pyramids were probably moved on rollers. Today, we still use rollers to help move goods more easily. Can you think where?

Something to try

Make your own rollers

You will need: some same-sized thread spools and a large, heavy book.

Place the spools on the table and put the book on top. Push the book forward with your hand. Can you discover any problems using rollers?

Usually, wheels are better than rollers because they stay attached to their load. No one knows exactly who invented the wheel, but in 3000 B.C. in Mesopotamia, solid wheels joined to a pole, called an axle, were being used. In about 1750 B.C., wheels with spokes were first used in Egypt. These were lighter than solid wheels, which meant that vehicles could move more easily.

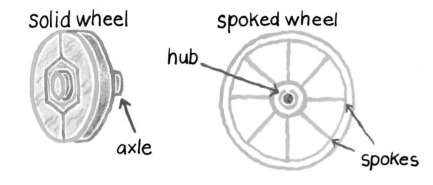

solid wheel

axle

spoked wheel

hub

spokes

ball bearings in a bicycle wheel

axle

Around 1000 B.C., wooden ball bearings were first used. These are small balls that separate the wheel from the axle so the wheel can spin freely. Today, wheels on most vehicles have steel ball bearings.

Something to try

Make your own ball bearings

You will need:
two aluminum cans with pry-off lids, a few marbles.

Rest one can upside down on top of the other and try to spin the top one around. Arrange a few marbles around the rim of the bottom tin and repeat the test. What happens?

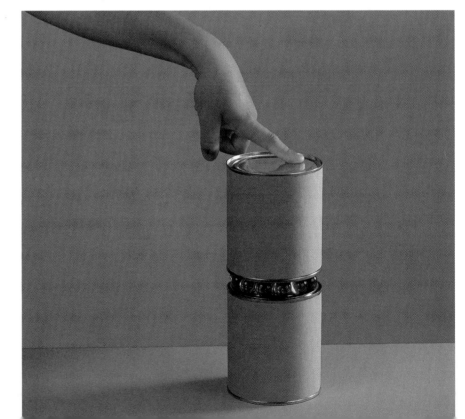

Friction can be useful when it stops things from traveling too quickly. Brakes on a bicycle press against part of the wheel and slow it down with friction. Brake drums in a car work in a similar way, but they press against the whole wheel.

Car tires grip the road, even in wet weather. The raised part of the tire, called the tread, scatters the water and holds on to the road. In winter, sand is spread on icy roads to make a rough surface for tires to grip. Some drivers even put chains over their tires to stop their cars from skidding on road snow and ice.

When our feet move too quickly for the rest of our body, we fall down. This can happen on a slippery floor or on ice. Rubber soles, thick treads, or spikes on our shoe soles can help keep us from falling.

Parachutes

Parachutists falling through the air need to slow down to break their fall. As they fall from the sky, gravity pulls them downward; at the same time, air is pushed inside the parachute and presses upward. This makes the parachute drift slowly to the ground.

Something to try

Make your own parachutes

You will need: small squares of different fabric cut the same size, some string, equal-sized balls of modeling clay, scissors, a stopwatch, some friends.

Cut four pieces of string the same length. Stick one end of each piece of string into a ball of clay. Tie the other ends of each piece of string to each of the four corners of a small fabric square. Make the other parachutes in the same way. Stand with the parachutes in your hand at the same height and drop them one at a time. Ask a friend to record how long each parachute takes to fall to the ground. Which parachute hits the ground first when you drop them all at the same time?

 P.S.   Make some small parachutes out of circles of fabric. What happens?

Streamlining

Today, cars travel much faster than the cars of the 1920s. New cars have better engines and most are streamlined. This means air passes easily over their smooth bodies, making very little air resistance. The shapc of a new car is tested in a wind tunnel. Smoky air is blown over the car, and the patterns in the smoke show how the car will cut through the air as the car moves along.

Rockets and aircraft are slim and sleek in shape; in water, the fastest speedboats have smooth, shiny hulls.

See which shapes dive the best

You will need:
a tall, clear jar or cylinder; modeling clay.

Divide the clay into pieces of the same size and make each one into a different shape. Make shapes you think will sink quickly in the container and others that will sink slowly. Which of your shapes reached the bottom first? Did you guess correctly?

Moving pictures

If you see two slightly different pictures very quickly one after the other, you may not notice that you have seen two pictures. Instead, you see one picture that appears to move. When you are shown twelve pictures per second, you will see them as separate pictures, but if you see the pictures faster than this, you see moving pictures. Movie films show you twenty-four photographs, or frames, per second.

Something to try

Make your own flicker book

You will need: a small notebook and a pencil.

On each page of the notebook, draw one of the pictures in this sequence. Each picture is slightly different from the one before. Make sure you draw only on the right-hand side of the page. Hold the notebook in one hand and flick the pages with the thumb on your other hand. In moving quickly, the pictures seem to move.

Draw a different sequence of pictures. Keep the pictures simple. Try drawing a stick-figure person dancing or bouncing a ball.

The speed of light

Light from the Sun travels through space to Earth at a speed of 186,000 miles (300,000 km) per second. At this speed, you could travel around Earth eight times in one second. It takes eight minutes for the light from the Sun to reach us. A racing car traveling nonstop at top speed would take about one hundred years to cover the same distance.

Light travels through water and glass more slowly than it does through air. When light rays travel from air into water, they bend at the surface. This is called refraction.

Something to try

See a pencil bend

Put some pencils in a glass of water. When you look at them, they appear bent because light from the pencils is distorted, or refracted; but when you lift them out of the water, they are straight.

The speed of sound

Sound travels through air more slowly than light. You see lightning before you hear thunder during a storm. Lightning and thunder happen at the same time, but we see lightning right away because light travels faster than sound. The sound waves from thunder take longer to reach our ears.

To find out how far away a storm is, count the number of seconds between the lightning flash and the sound of thunder. Divide your answer by three. This is the storm's approximate distance from you in kilometers. To get the distance in miles, divide by five. The farther away the storm is, the longer it will take for the sound of thunder to reach you.

An echo is a sound that bounces back and can be heard again.
When you shout at a rock face or a wall some distance away,
you can sometimes hear an echo. A short time passes before
you hear the echo because the sound waves travel at about
1,083 feet (330 m) per second.

Something to try

Measure the speed of sound

You will need:
two spoons, a wall, a stopwatch, the help of a friend.

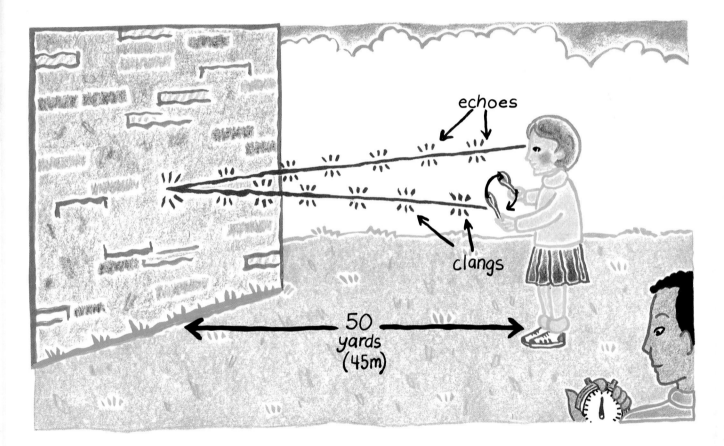

Stand 50 yards (45 m) from a large wall. Clang two metal spoons
together loudly and wait for the echo. As soon as you hear the echo,
clang the spoons again. Try to clang in an even rhythm, clang, echo,
clang, echo. Ask a friend to time 100 of your clangs with a stopwatch.
Between each clang, sound travels to and from the wall, so it travels
100 yards (91 m). After 100 clangs, the sound has traveled 100 x 100
yards (10,000 yards or 9,144 m). Speed is the distance covered in a
certain time. So if you divide 10,000 by the time it took you to make
100 clangs, you will have the approximate speed of sound.

Speed of life

As technology advances, so does the speed at which we do things. In medieval times, a trip of a few hundred miles (km) could take several weeks on foot or on horseback. In the eighteenth century, horse-drawn carriages could travel the same distance in several days. In the nineteenth century, steam locomotives were invented, making the trip even faster. The picture at right shows George Stephenson's locomotive, *The Rocket*. Today, high-speed trains (below) can travel at over 100 miles (160 km) per hour.

GEO. STEPHENSON'S ROCKET, 1829.

In medieval times, scrolls and books were handwritten and took years to complete. By the fifteenth century, the first European mechanical printing press had been invented, and books could be printed in a few weeks. Today, millions of newspapers with up-to-date information can be prepared and printed overnight.

Can you think of some inventions that have helped speed up our way of life?

Important events

3000 B.C.   In Mesopotamia, solid wheels joined to an axle were being used.

1750 B.C.   In Egypt, spoked wheels were being used.

1000 B.C.   In Europe, wooden ball bearings were being used to help wheels turn more easily.

490 B.C.   An athlete ran 24.85 miles (40 km) from Marathon to Athens. A long-distance race, the marathon, is named after this event.

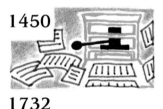

1450   In Germany, Johannes Gutenberg invented the printing press. He was able to produce three hundred printed pages each day. In Europe, printed books gradually replaced handwritten books.

1732   Henri Pitot invented the Pitot tube, which measured water pressure. Later, the tube was adapted to measure air pressure. Today, the Pitot tube is used to help measure the speed of aircraft.

1832   One of the first methods of producing moving pictures was invented.

1932   Amelia Earhart was the first woman to make a solo flight over the Atlantic Ocean. She flew from Newfoundland to Ireland.

1969   Three U.S. astronauts flew at the speed of 24,792 miles (39,897 km) per hour during the Apollo 10 mission, the fastest speed at which people have traveled.

1983   Richard Noble set a new land-speed record of 633.497 miles (1,019.467 km) per hour in his rocket-driven car, *Thrust 2*.

1987   The fastest passenger train in the world was clocked at 247.6 miles (398.4 km) per hour on its route in Japan.

1993   Noureddine Morceli of Algeria set a world record by running a mile (1.6 km) in 3.44 minutes.

For more information

More things to do

1. Five minutes is one-twelfth of an hour. If you take the number of yards (m) that you walk in 5 minutes and multiply it by 12, you will find the number of yards (m) that you would walk in one hour.

2. Find out who holds the world record for the 100-meter dash. If this athlete could keep up this speed for longer, approximately how long would it take him or her to run 1 kilometer?

3. Use a map, atlas, or other reference to determine the distance between your home and another city in your state or an adjacent state. If you were to maintain a speed of 60 miles (96 km) per hour while traveling to this city, approximately how long would it take you to get there?

4. Speed skaters can cover 500 meters in less than 40 seconds during a race. How do speed skaters try to reduce the effects of gravity and wind resistance, thereby enabling them to travel at faster speeds? Do you see any similarities in the streamlining done in car design, as shown on page 22?

5. Study food packaging to see if any of the manufacturers use the "speed" of preparation as a selling point for the product. How many products can you find in the supermarket that promise to be "fast" to prepare? On the other hand, do any products boast about "slow" and careful preparation (e.g. "hours in the oven") before packaging that add to the quality? How does the concept of speed enter into the choices consumers make while shopping for food?

More books to read

Animal Olympians. Thone Maynard (Franklin Watts)
Built to Speed. Jonathon Rutland (Random)
Clocks, Scales, and Measurement. Pam Robson (Gloucester Press)
The Fastest and Slowest. Anita Ganeri (Barron's)
How Science Works. Judith Hann (Dorling Kindersley)
Making Metric Measurements. Neil Ardley (Franklin Watts)
Time, Distance, and Speed. Marion Smoothey (Marshall Cavendish)
Weights and Measures. Robin Kerrod (Marshall Cavendish)
World's Fastest Motorcycles. John Martin (Capstone Press)

Videotapes

Forces and Motion. (Children's Television Workshop)
How Speedometers Work. (Films for the Humanities and Sciences)
Measuring Is Important. (Barr Films)

Places to visit

Museum of Science and Industry
57th Street and Lake Shore Drive
Chicago, IL 60637

Indianapolis Motor Speedway Museum
4790 West 16th Street
Indianapolis, IN 46222

National Museum of Science and Technology
1867 Saint Laurent Boulevard
Ottawa, Ontario K1G 5A3

Science World
1455 Quebec Street
Vancouver, British Columbia V6A 3Z7

Index

For a free color catalog describing Gareth Stevens' list of high-quality books, call 1-800-542-2595 (USA) or 1-800-461-9120 (Canada). Gareth Stevens' Fax: (414) 225-0377.

Library of Congress Cataloging-in-Publication Data available upon request from publisher.
Fax: (414) 225-0377 for the attention of the Publishing Records Department.

ISBN 0-8368-1362-6

This edition first published in 1995 by
Gareth Stevens Publishing
1555 North RiverCenter Drive, Suite 201
Milwaukee, Wisconsin 53212, USA

This edition © 1995 by Gareth Stevens, Inc. Original edition published in 1992 by A & C Black (Publishers) Ltd., 35 Bedford Row, London WC1R 4JH.

© 1992 A & C Black (Publishers) Ltd. Additional end matter © 1995 by Gareth Stevens, Inc.

Acknowledgements
Photographs by Chris Fairclough, except for: p. 2 Paul Ridsdale, CFCL; pp. 3 (b), 6, 10, 11 (b), 16 (t), 20, 28 (b), 29 (l) CFCL; p. 4 (t) John Cox, CFCL; p. 4 (b) Michael Holford; p. 5 (t) Bruce Coleman; p. 7 Allsport; p. 8 National Maritime Museum; p. 17 Mike Morton, CFCL; p. 21 (l) John Davies, CFCL; p. 22 Ford Motor Company; p. 26 Jon Arnold, CFCL; p. 28 (t) Mary Evans Picture Library; p. 29 (r) The Hulton Picture Company; main cover photo Graham Taylor, CFCL.

Printed in Mexico
1 2 3 4 5 6 7 8 9 99 98 97 96 95